Usborne English Readers

Level 1

The Ugly Duckling

Retold by Laura Cowan

Illustrated by Alexandra Badiu

English language consultant: Peter Viney

Contents

You can listen to the story online here:
usborne.com/uglyducklingaudio

It was a lovely sunny day on the farm. Ducks were swimming on the pond, but one mother duck couldn't swim with them. She had to sit on her eggs. "When are they going to hatch?" she thought.

She waited and waited, and finally they
did. Pretty yellow ducklings ran this way
and that, but the biggest egg didn't hatch.

"What a beautiful family," an old duck
said to the mother.

"Hmm, thank you... but why isn't the
biggest egg hatching?" she asked.

"Let me see," said the old duck.
"It's very big. Maybe it's a turkey's egg."

"I'm going to sit on it some more,"
said the mother duck.

That afternoon, the egg broke open.

Slowly a beak came out, and then a
duckling. He wasn't a nice yellow like his
brothers and sisters. His beak was black
and he looked dirty. He was clumsy, too.
His feet were too big and his wings were
too short.

The mother duck thought, "Well, he
is very big and he looks very different.
Maybe he *is* a turkey."

The next day, the mother duck said to
her family, "Let's go swimming!" All the
ducklings ran and jumped into the pond.
The biggest duckling ran after them.

Soon they were all swimming happily.
The biggest duckling enjoyed the
swimming, too.

"He's not a turkey!" the mother duck
said. "He can swim very well – and in the
water he's not clumsy! Now I can show
my ducklings to the other farm birds."

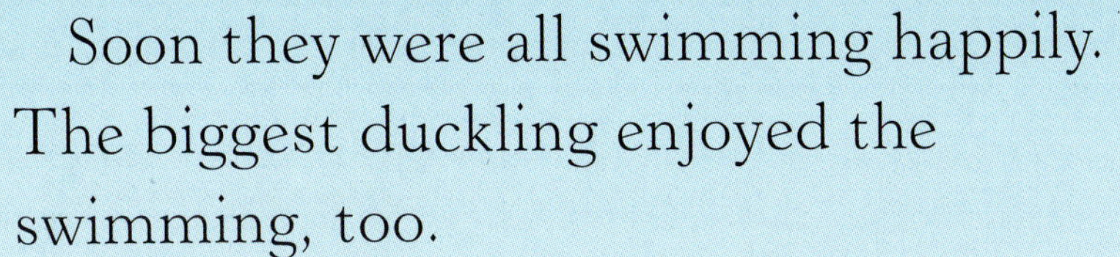

The mother duck took her new family
to the farmyard. Lots of birds lived there.
There were more ducks and hens, and a
big old turkey, too. They all came to look
at the ducklings.

"Ooh, what an ugly duckling!" one said.
"Why is he different from the others?"
She flapped her wings.

The duckling ran to hide behind
his mother.

"Don't do that!" The mother duck was angry. "He's frightened. Can't you see?"

"Ha, what is he? He isn't a duck. We don't want him here," said the old turkey.

"Maybe he isn't as pretty as the others," said the mother duck, "but he has a good heart, and he can swim very well."

The turkey laughed. "Well, *I'm* the most important bird in the farmyard, and *I* don't want him."

After that, the duckling couldn't enjoy anything. He had no friends in the farmyard. When the farm girl gave the birds their food, the duckling ate his last.

Even his brothers and sisters didn't
like him. They all laughed at him. "All I
can do is swim," he thought. "They don't
laugh at me when I'm swimming."

Finally the duckling ran away from the
farm. He loved his mother and she loved
him, but he was so unhappy.

That night he slept by the road. When
he woke up, it was raining. It rained and
rained. It was the end of summer.

The duckling started walking. "Maybe I can find some friends on another farm," he thought. Then he heard a man's loud voice. "What's that? Bring it here, Rudi!" A brown dog ran up to the duckling with its mouth open. "My life is over," the duckling thought.

The dog stopped and looked surprised. "I don't want to catch you. You're much too ugly!"

"Well, sometimes being ugly isn't a bad thing," thought the duckling.

He walked on through the fields. He was so cold and tired. Finally he saw a small house. "Maybe they are nice here," he thought.

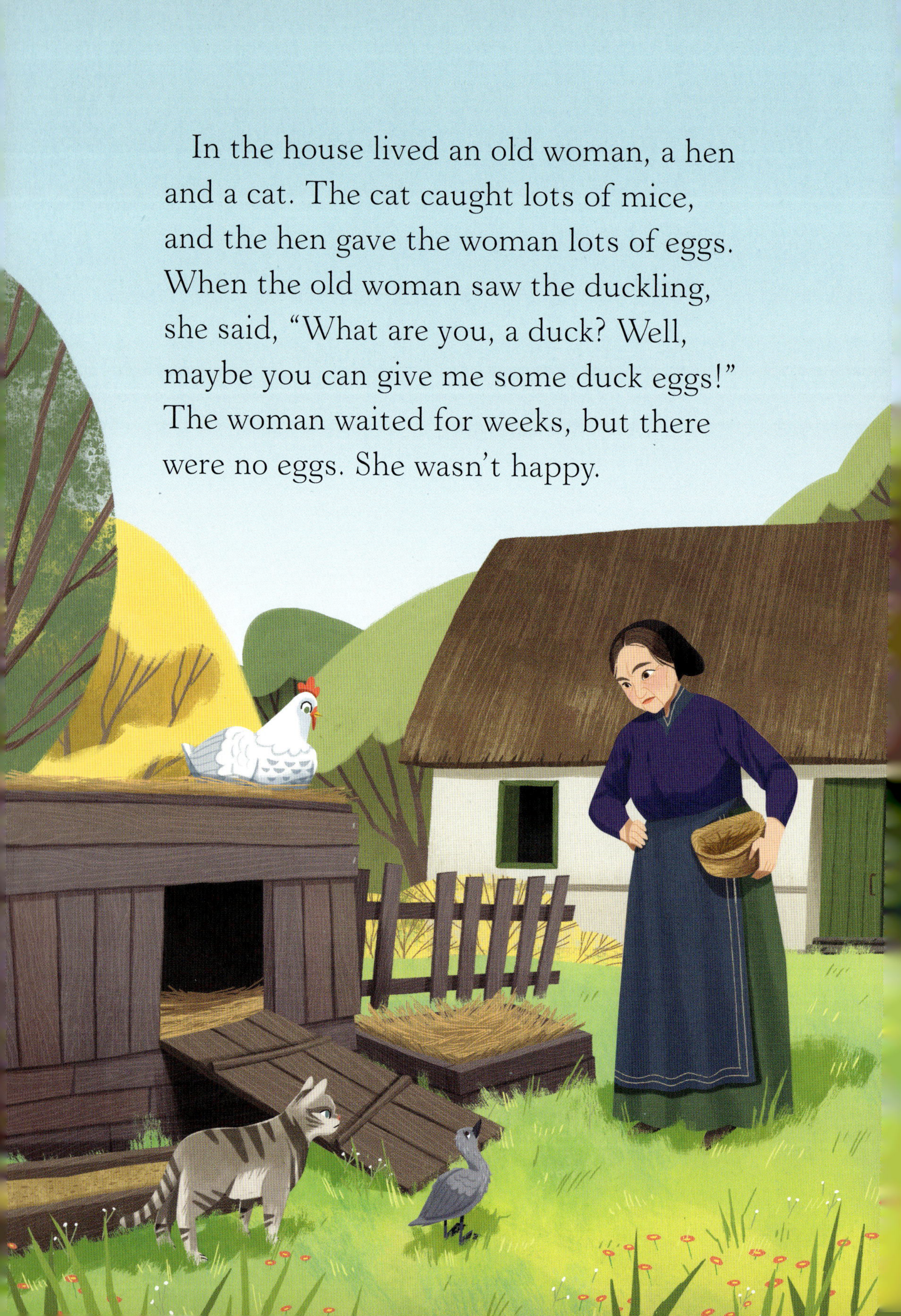

In the house lived an old woman, a hen and a cat. The cat caught lots of mice, and the hen gave the woman lots of eggs. When the old woman saw the duckling, she said, "What are you, a duck? Well, maybe you can give me some duck eggs!" The woman waited for weeks, but there were no eggs. She wasn't happy.

"I can't do anything useful," thought the duckling sadly. "I have to leave." He went out into the fields again.

After a few days, he found a pond. "I can go swimming!" he thought. He swam and swam, and he felt much better.

There were other ducks on the pond, but the duckling was frightened of them. He didn't go near them.

One day, the duckling saw some white birds on the pond. They were swans, tall and lovely with long thin necks. They swam beautifully.

"They are like kings and queens! Who are they?" thought the duckling. He wanted to know, but he couldn't ask. None of the other birds liked him. How could the swans be his friends?

Soon the beautiful birds flapped their big white wings and flew up, up, into the sky.

"Oh!" the duckling cried. They were gone and he felt strange. "I can't forget them. They were so lovely," he thought.

It was winter now. All the other ducks
flew away, but not the duckling. Where
could he go? The pond was very cold. The
water froze a little more each day until
the duckling couldn't move. He stayed
there all night.

In the morning, a farmer saw him in the
frozen water. "Funny little bird! You can
come home with me," he said. He took
the duckling to his house and put him
next to the kitchen fire.

The duckling was happy, but then the
farmer's children came home from school.
"Catch him!" they laughed. The duckling
was frightened of their games. He ran
and hid under a chair, but they soon
found him.

"Come out, little bird!" they said. "We
want to play with you!" The duckling ran
out of the door and into the cold again.

Weeks passed, and then months.
The duckling had a terrible time. He was
always cold and hungry. He couldn't swim
because the ponds were frozen. He slept
in the fields.

One morning he woke up, and there was
no wind or rain. The sun was warm on his
body. Finally, the long winter was over.

The duckling flapped his wings. They were much bigger and stronger now. He could fly! He flew up into the blue sky. He flew above a house with a garden. There were trees and flowers and a big pond. On the pond were beautiful birds with long, thin necks and big, white wings.

"It's them!" thought the duckling,
"I'm going to fly down, even if they swim
away from me. I have to meet them." He
flew down to the pond. He put his head
down and looked in the water. What did
he see? Not a big clumsy duckling, but
a beautiful swan! The other swans swam
around him.

"Hello! You're one of us!" they said, and
they touched his neck with their beaks.
The young swan didn't know what to say.
He was so happy.

Some children ran into the garden. They had food for the swans. The young swan wasn't frightened now. He ate happily.

"Oh look, there's a new one!" said the youngest child. "I think he's the most beautiful of them all."

About Hans Christian Andersen

Hans Christian Andersen lived in Denmark over 100 years ago. His family was very poor. When he was a child, he didn't have many friends, but he loved stories.

In 1837, Andersen wrote a book of stories for children. It was very popular, and Andersen wrote many more stories between 1838-1872. Some other stories by Andersen are *The Emperor's New Clothes*, *The Little Mermaid*, *The Snow Queen* and *The Emperor and the Nightingale*.

Andersen felt very much like the Ugly Duckling in real life. He was unhappy as a child, and he felt very different from his family and other people in his home town of Odense. He moved to the city of Copenhagen when he was 14. After more unhappy years at school, he started writing. He finally became famous and successful with his stories for children.

Activities

The answers are on page 32.

What an ugly duckling!
Which of these sentences are true?

A.
He isn't a nice yellow like his brothers and sisters.

B.
He is a turkey.

C.
He can swim very well.

D.
His brothers and sisters love him.

E.
He runs away from the farm.

F.
He can give the old woman duck eggs.

G.
He can't forget the swans.

What happened when?

Can you put these pictures and sentences
in the right order?

A.

One day, the duckling
saw some white birds
on the pond.

B.

The biggest duckling
enjoyed the swimming,
too.

C.

He put his head
down and looked
in the water.

D.

The turkey didn't
want the duckling
on the farm.

E.

"When are they going
to hatch?"

F.

A brown dog ran up
to the duckling with
its mouth open.

What are they like?

Choose the right words to finish the sentences.

beautiful   hungry   nice   silly

tired   ugly   unhappy   wet

1.

He was so ....

2.

He was so ....

"I don't want to catch you.
You're much too ...."

3.

"Maybe they are .... here."

4.

The .... birds flew up,
up into the sky.

What does the ugly duckling want?

Choose the right thought for each picture.

1.

2.

3.

4.

The end of the story

One word in each sentence is wrong.
Can you choose the right word?

1. There were trees and flowers and a big field.

2. The children had water for the swans.

3. The old swan wasn't frightened now.

4. The new house was the most beautiful of them all.

Word list

beak (n) a bird's mouth and nose are in its beak.

clumsy (adj) if you don't move carefully, and you hit things or break things, you are clumsy.

duck (n) a bird that lives on or near water. Some ducks live on farms. There are also wild ducks.

enjoy (v) when you enjoy something, you like it and it makes you happy.

farmyard (n) the space in the middle of farm buildings. There are often ducks and hens in a farmyard.

field (n) on a farm, you grow food or keep animals in fields.

finally (adv) at the end of a long time.

flap (v) when birds flap their wings, they move them quickly up and down.

freeze, froze (v), **frozen** (adj) when water is very cold, it freezes and turns into ice.